Frogs Dream

Written and Illustrated by
Rachel Marolf Chouteau

Archway Publishing books may be ordered through booksellers or by contacting:

Archway Publishing
1663 Liberty Drive
Bloomington, IN 47403
www.archwaypublishing.com
1 (888) 242-5904

ISBN: 978-1-4808-2295-5 (sc)
ISBN: 978-1-4808-2296-2 (e)

Print information available on the last page.

Archway Publishing rev. date: 10/12/2015

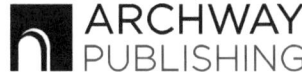

ARCHWAY
PUBLISHING

Dream, frogs, dream
And you can make
A lovely, frosted
Layer-cake.

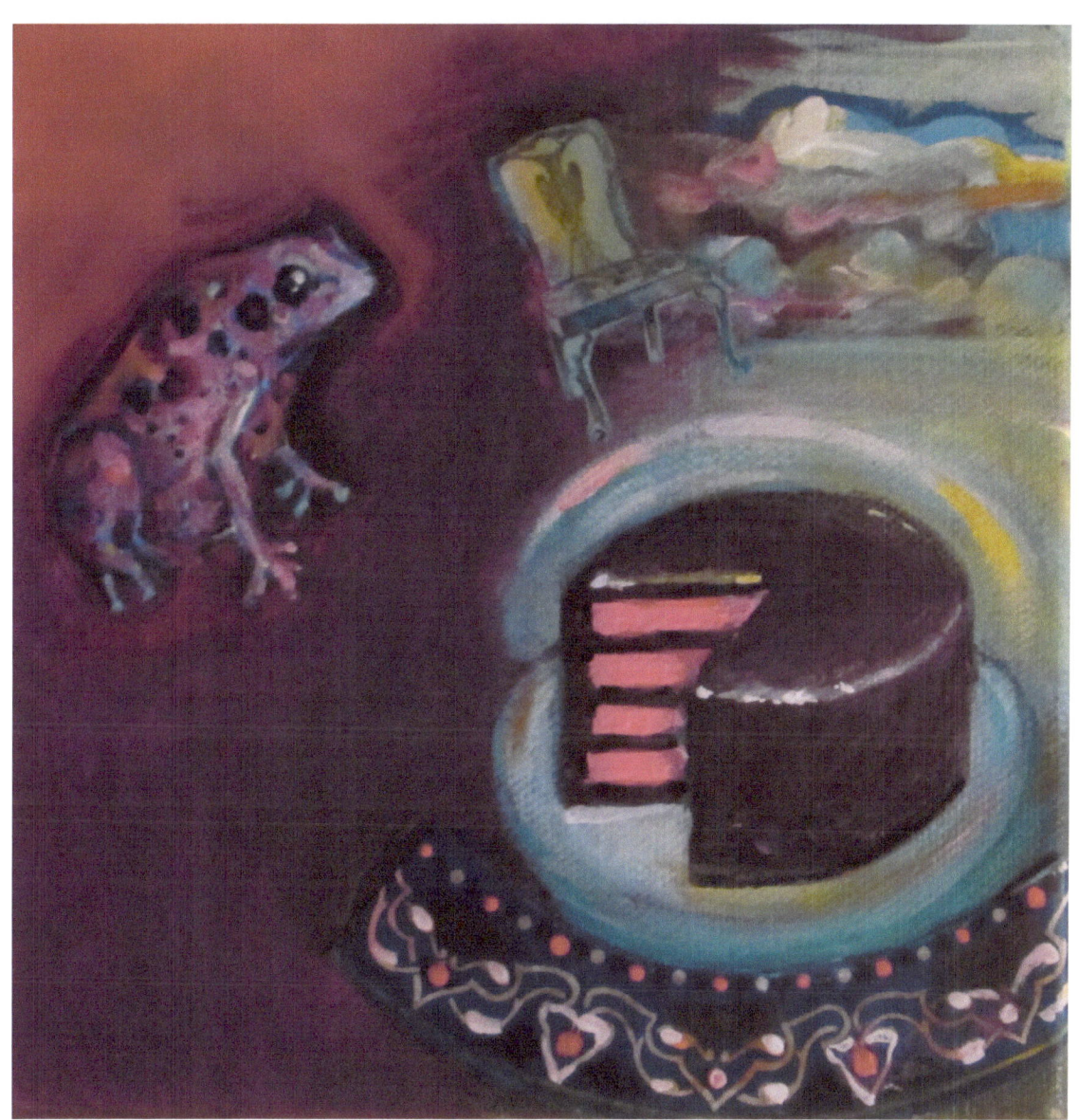

Holy Genache

Dream, frogs, dream
And you can fly
With Kiskadee
Up in the sky.

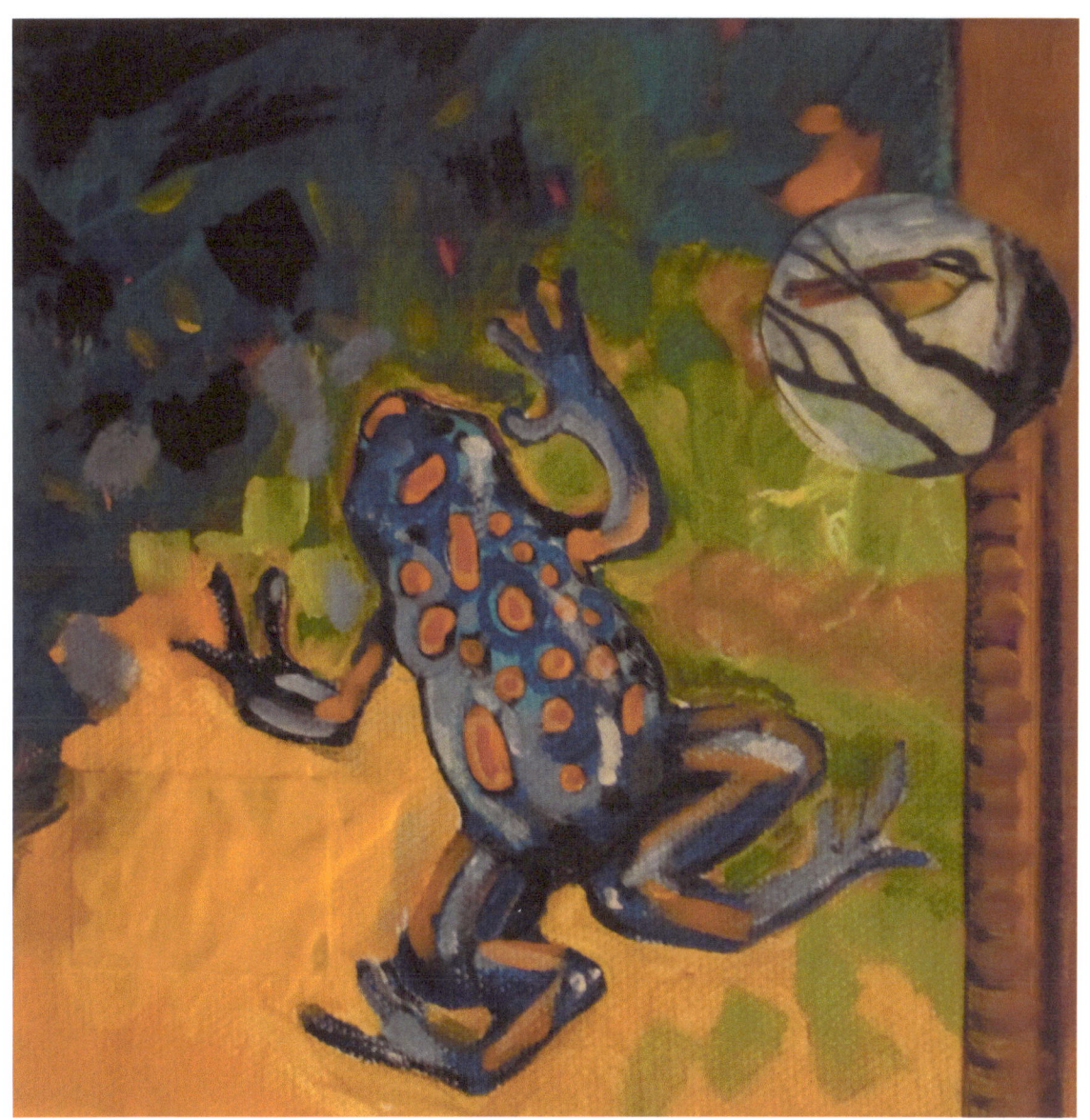

Birdie, Bird

Dream, frogs, dream
And you can play
Sweet music
On a sunny day.

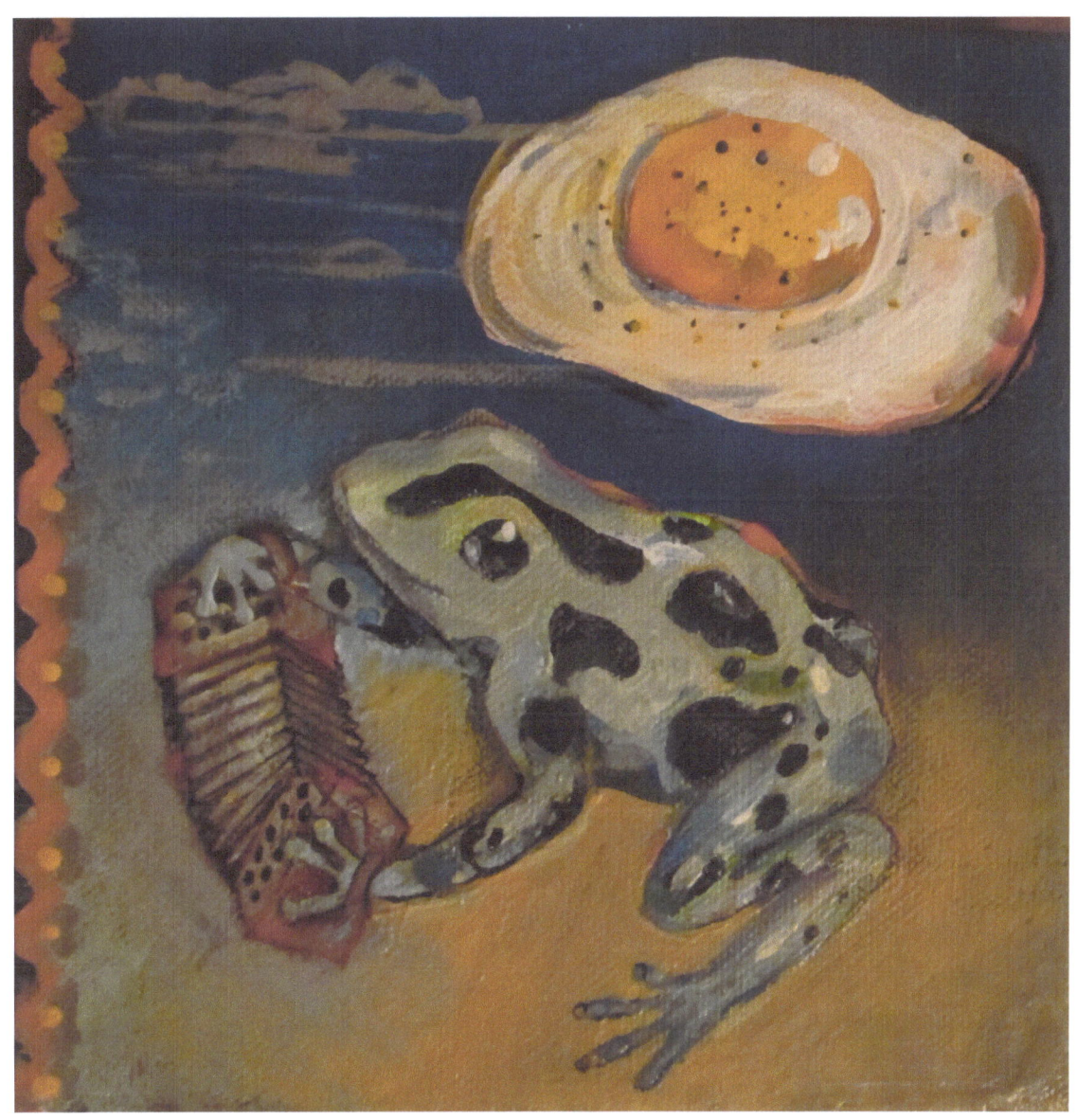

Eggshine

Dream, frogs, dream
And you'll surprise
A favorite friend
While in disguise.

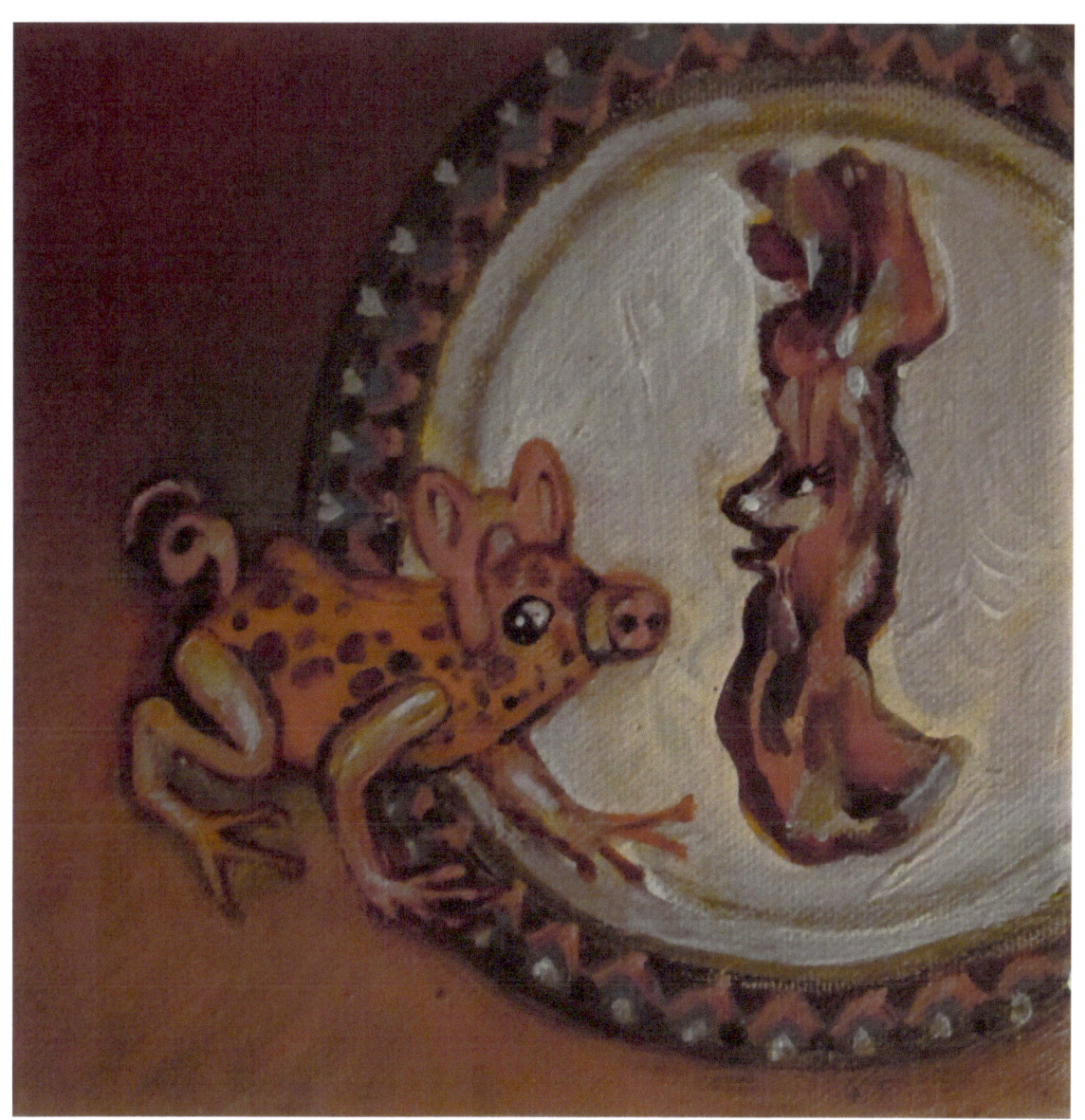

Oink, Oink

Dream, frogs, dream
And you can tell
Miss Mermaid likes you
Very well.

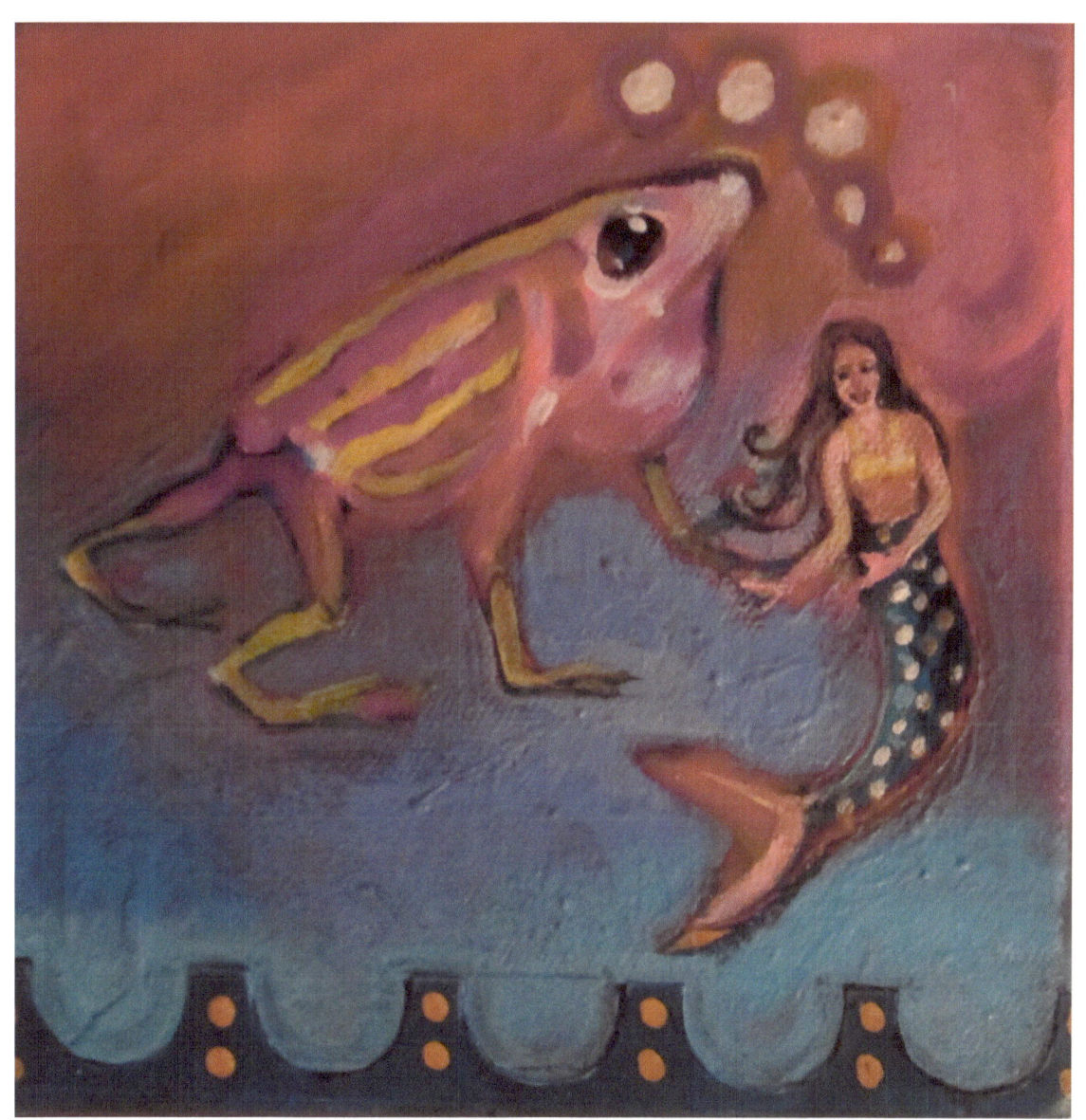

Stripes of Gold

Dream, frogs, dream
And dance so fine
The stars above will
Shine, shine, shine.

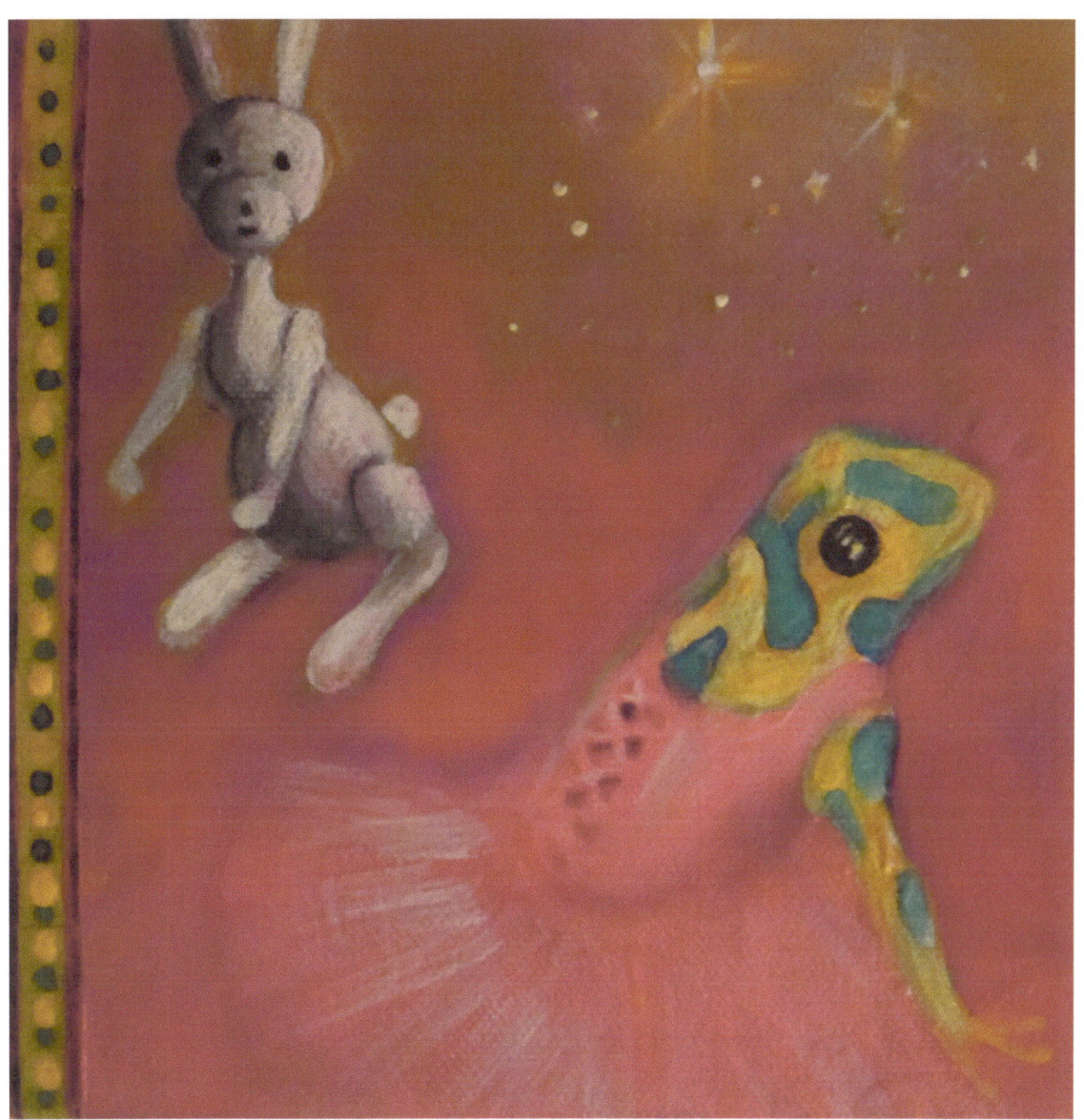

Twinkle, Twinkle

Dream, frogs, dream
And you can be
An acrobat
Quite gracefully.

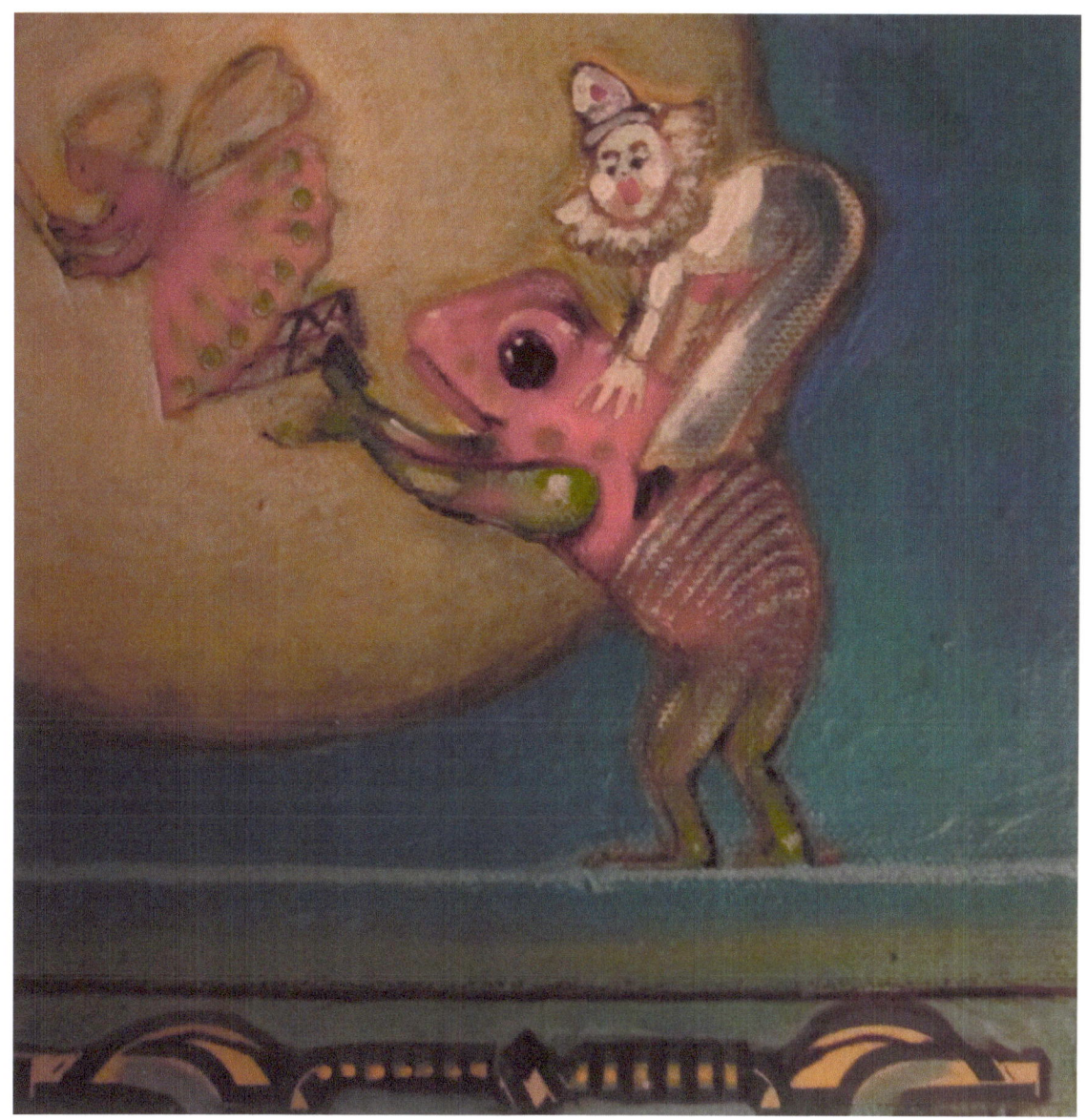

Circus Act

Dream, frogs, dream
And you can eat
A chocolate cupcake.
What a treat!

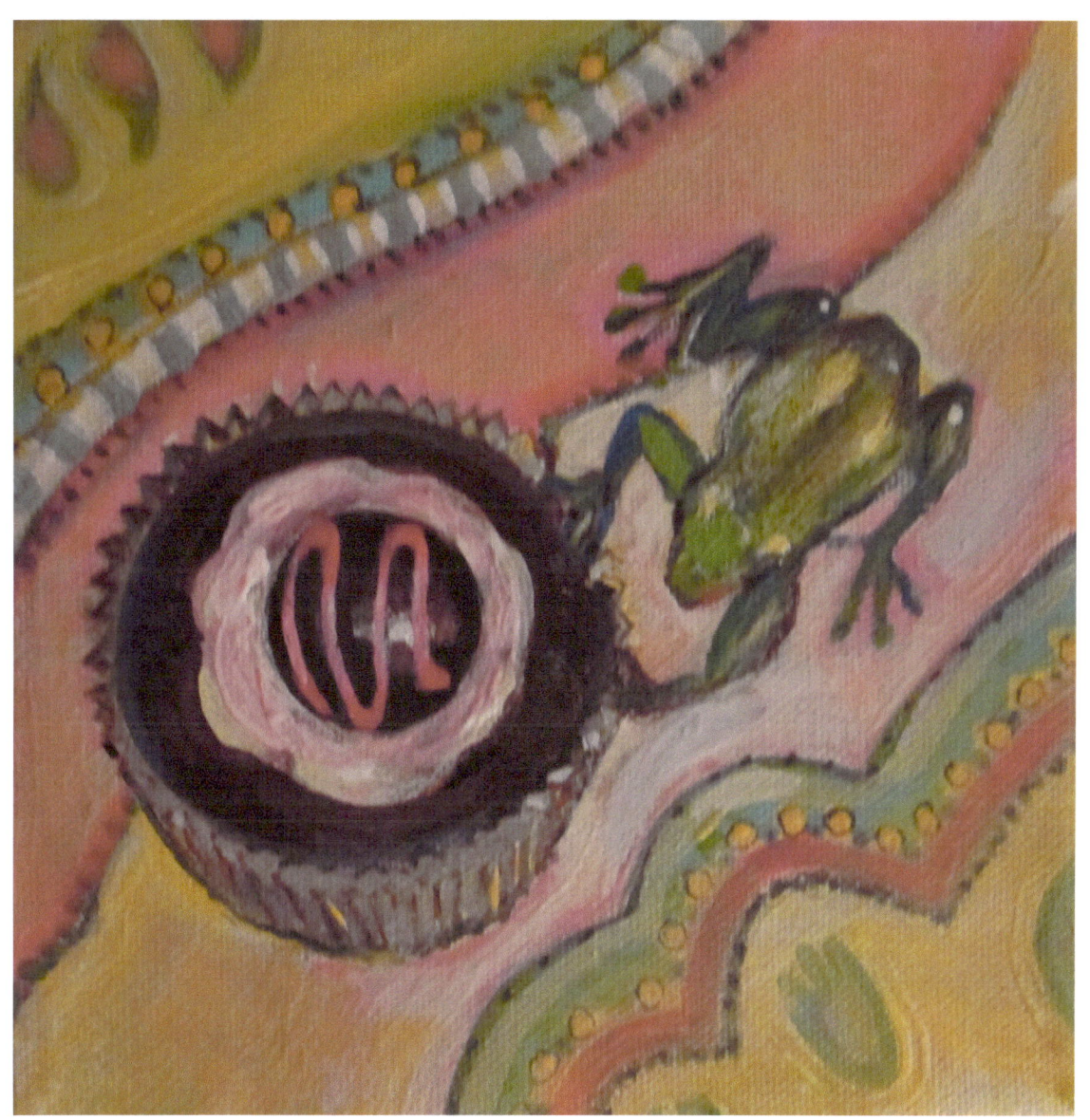

Hello, Cupcake

Dream, frogs, dream
And you can try
To touch the moon
Way, way up high.

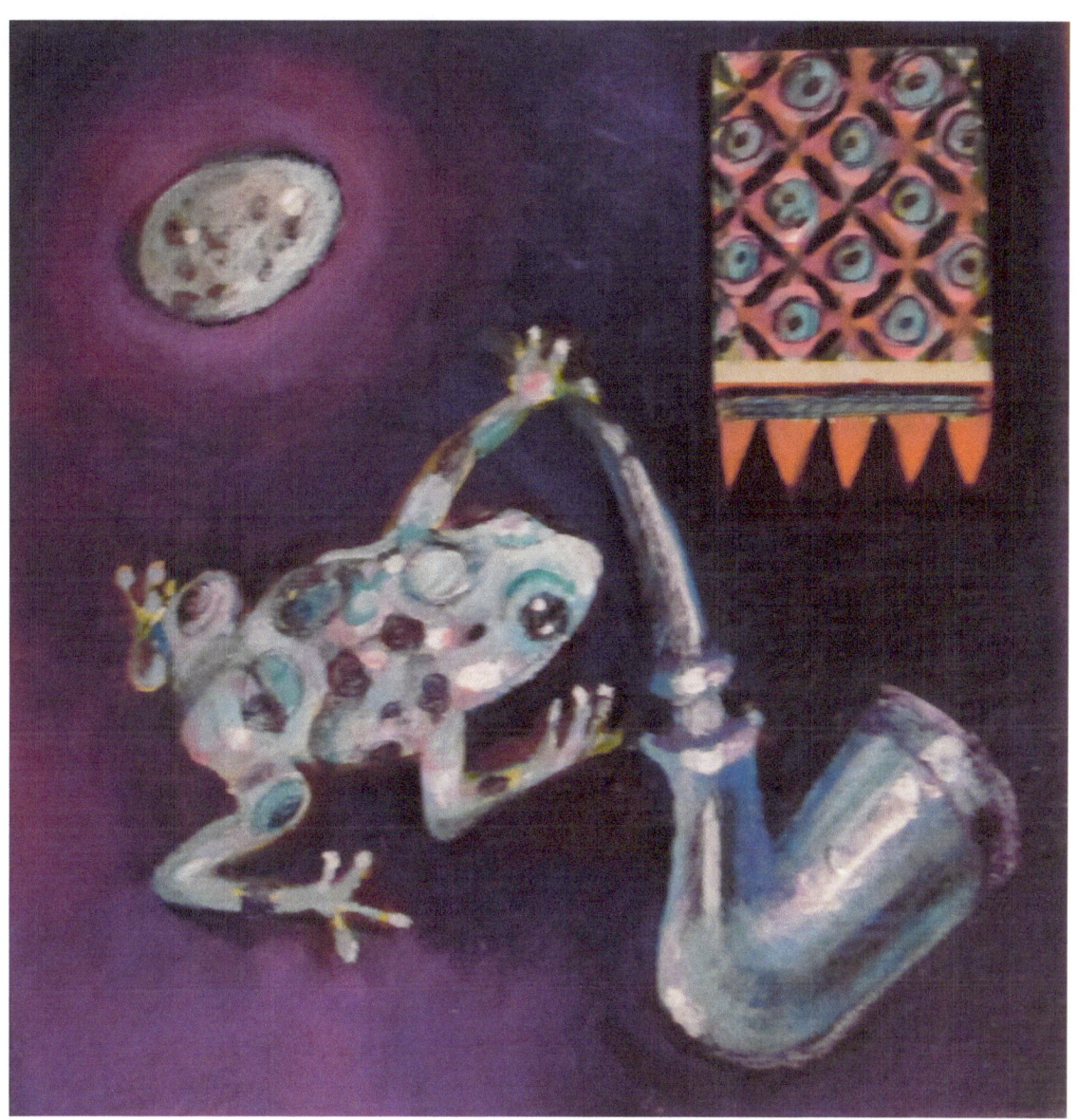

Under the Eggmoon

Dream, frogs, dream
Of shiny things
And you can wear
A flashy ring.

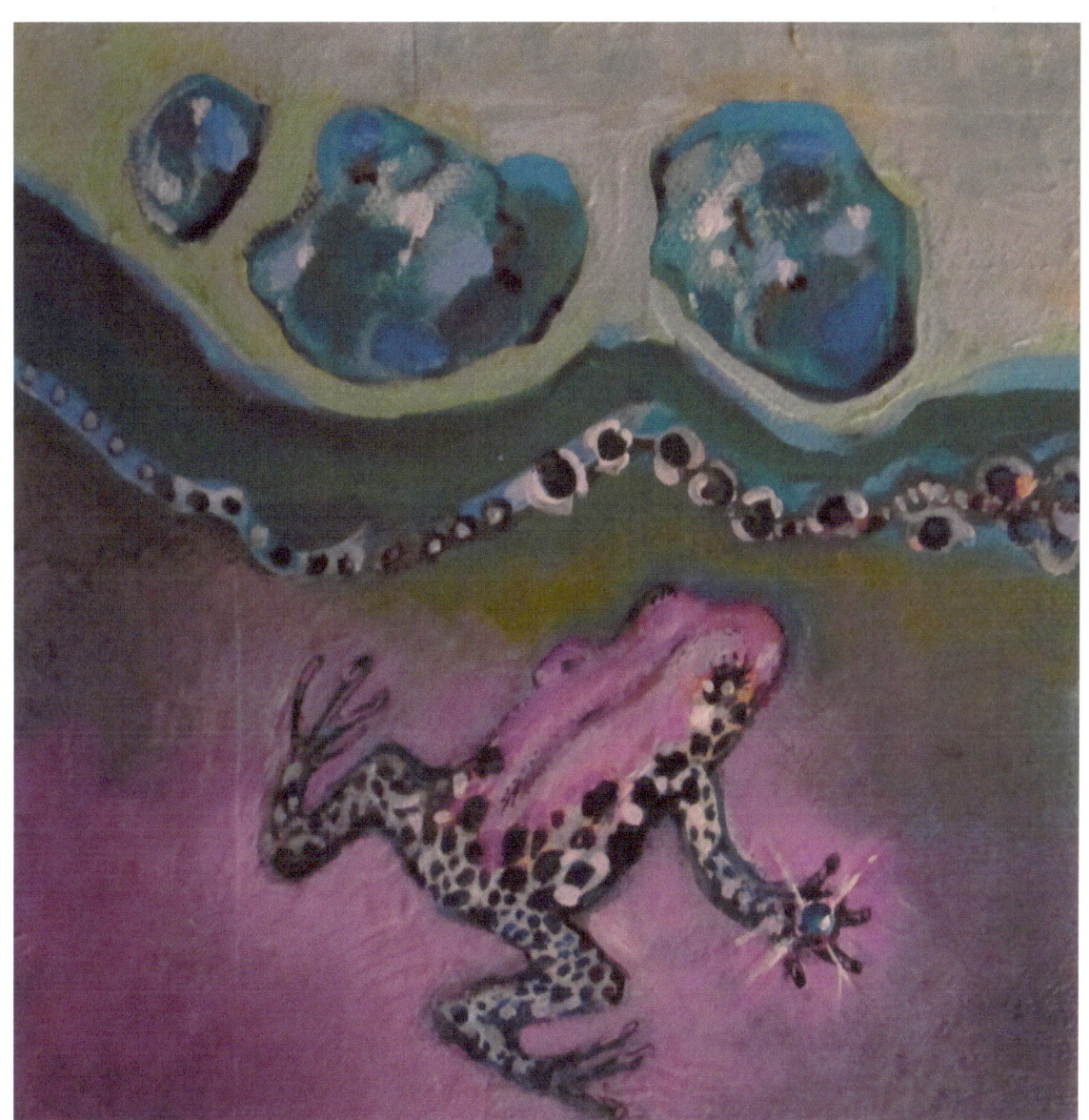

Turquoise Rocks

Dream, frogs, dream
And you can hop
Up to a lovely
Mountaintop

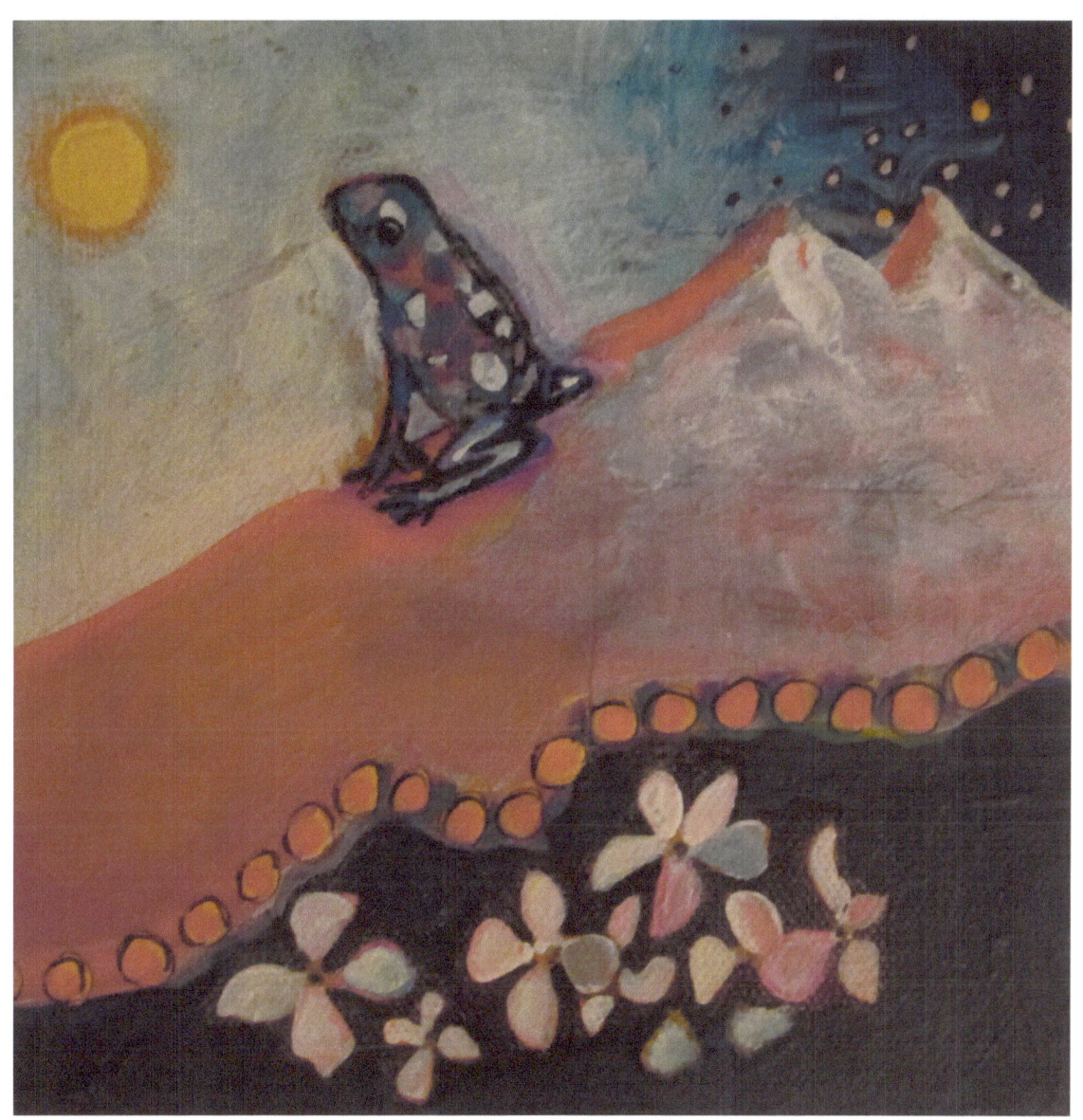

Dreamer

Dream, frogs, dream
And you can put
A shoe of gold
On every foot.

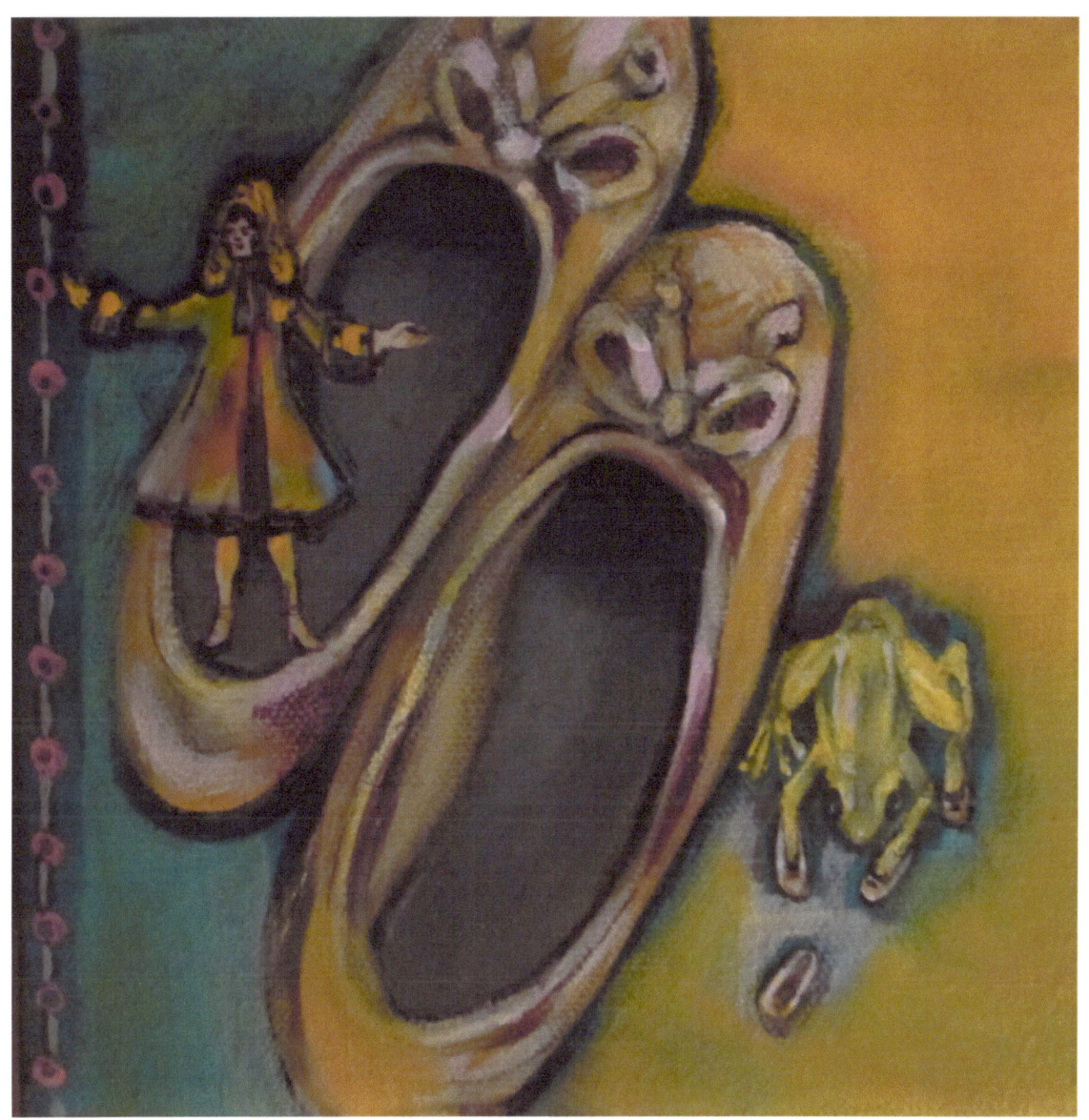

Tiny Toes

Dream, frogs, dream
Of things you'll do
And someday soon
Dreams may come true.

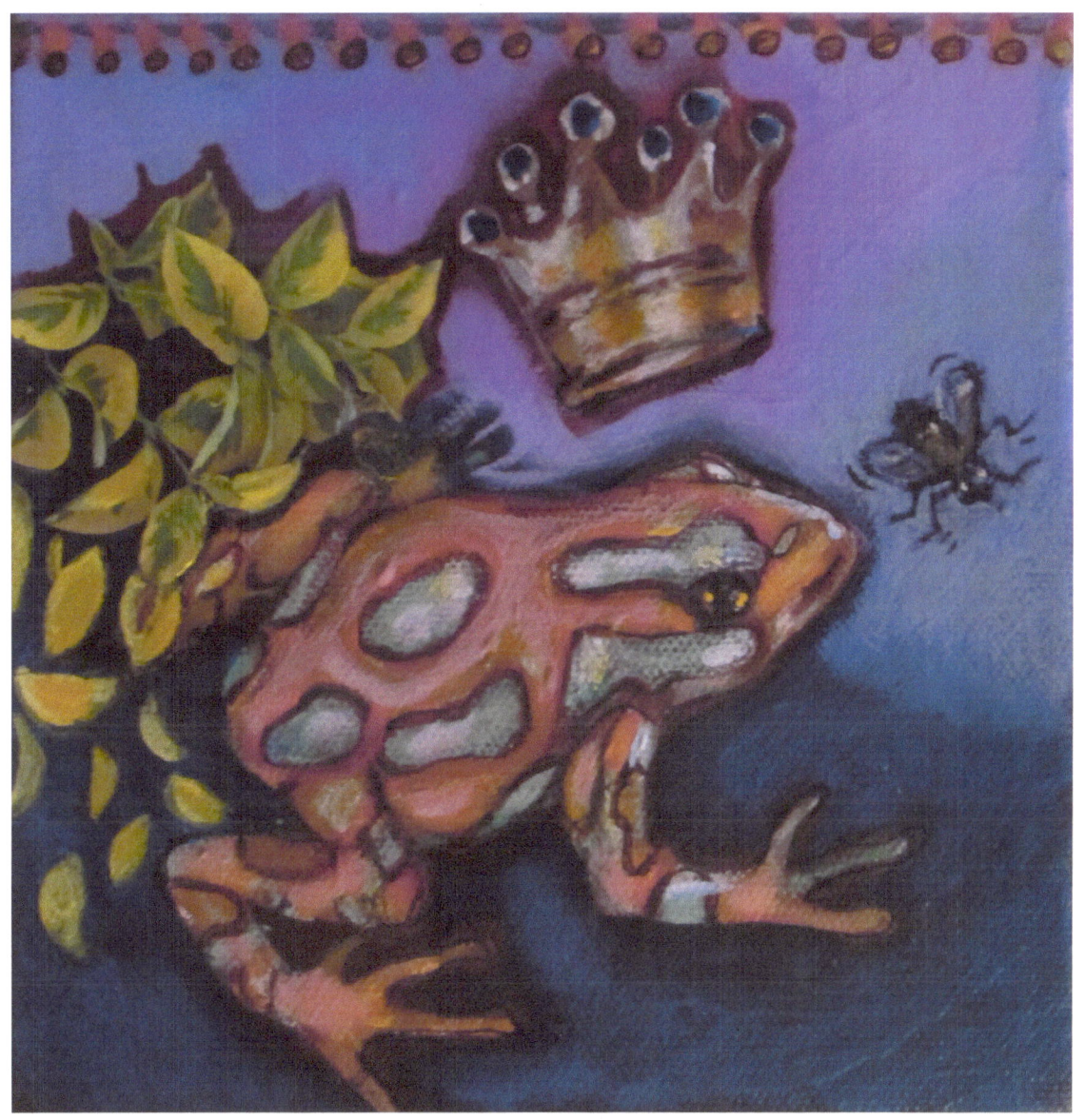

Kiss Me, You Fool

www.ingramcontent.com/pod-product-compliance
Lightning Source LLC
Chambersburg PA
CBHW040308010626
45792CB00025B/1694